The World's Best Maggie Thatcher Jokes

Des MacHale

Illustrated by Hugh Linehan

ANGUS
& ROBERTSON
PUBLISHERS

ANGUS & ROBERTSON PUBLISHERS

Unit 4, Eden Park, 31 Waterloo Road,
North Ryde, NSW, Australia 2113, and
16 Golden Square, London W1R 4BN,
United Kingdom

First published in the United Kingdom by
Angus & Robertson (UK) in 1989
First published in Australia by
Angus & Robertson Publishers in 1989
Reprinted 1989, 1990

Copyright © Des MacHale, 1989
Illustrations © Hugh Linehan, 1989

British Library Cataloguing in Publication Data
MacHale, Des
    The world's best Maggie Thatcher jokes
    I. Title.
    828'.91402
ISBN 0 207 16224 7

Typeset by New Faces, Bedford
Printed by BPCC Hazell Books, Aylesbury

The World's Best Maggie Thatcher Jokes

Foreword

This, to the best of my knowledge, is the first definitive book of Margaret Thatcher jokes ever to be published, though some will dispute this claim, recalling recent Conservative election manifestos. Britain is the land of private enterprise yet no private has had the enterprise to produce a side-splitting volume of Maggie jokes such as this – it had to be left to an Irishman.

Denis Thatcher gets a mention here and there too in this book and even Mark Thatcher gets his nose into one or two little jokes. However, even a careful search will uncover no jokes about Mrs Thatcher's daughter Carol . . .

– Des MacHale

Here's to the Iron Lady – may she rust in peace!

Margaret Thatcher boasts that Britain is one of the few really stable countries. Well, you know what's mostly found in stables ...

Denis Thatcher was playing a round of golf with some friends when he rushed up to the foursome in front of them and addressed them with an anxious look on his face.

'I say, I wonder would you chaps mind awfully if we play through? I've just had an urgent message that my wife has been taken seriously ill.'

Margaret Thatcher did for women's liberation what the Boston strangler did for door-to-door salesmen.

Three British politicians were allowed to address God and ask Him a single question.

'When will the Labour Party get back in government?' asked the leader of the Labour Party.

'In twenty years,' God answered, so the Labour Party leader burst into tears and went away crying.

'When will the SDP get into government?' asked the SDP leader.

'In a hundred years,' answered God, so the SDP leader burst into tears and went away crying.

'When will my policies solve the unemployment problem?' asked Margaret Thatcher and God burst into tears and went away crying.

An old psychiatrist died and made his way to the pearly gates.

'Thank heavens you've come,' said St Peter. 'We've got a real crisis on our hands – God thinks He's Margaret Thatcher.'

Margaret Thatcher and her ministers have just come up with a fantastic new scheme to shorten the dole queues – they're going to line them up four deep.

Most Tory ministers can never get over the embarrassing fact that they were born in bed with a woman.

Margaret Thatcher was at an international conference when she was introduced to two gentlemen – the Swiss Minister for the Navy and the Russian Minister for Private Enterprise.

'That's amusing,' she chuckled, 'Switzerland doesn't have any sea boundaries and Russia doesn't have any private enterprise.'

'Maybe so,' smiled one of them, 'but haven't you got a Ministry for Employment?'

Denis Thatcher went into a bookshop and asked the assistant, 'Do you have a book called "How to Control your Wife"?'

'Our fiction section is upstairs sir,' smiled the assistant.

A thought to ponder – the taxes an average tax-payer pays in a lifetime are spent by Margaret Thatcher's government in five seconds.

Margaret Thatcher and Denis were on an ocean voyage when the ship sank and the pair of them wound up on a lifeboat in the middle of the ocean with no water or provisions. They drifted helplessly for a week and were about to give up hope when they saw land on the horizon. Feebly they rowed towards it and as they neared the shore they saw a crowd of people gathered round a scaffold where a man was about to be hanged. 'Oh, thank heavens, Denis,' cried Margaret Thatcher, 'it's a Christian country.'

Contrary to what many people think, Margaret Thatcher has absolutely nothing against coloured people. In fact, she thinks everyone should own one.

Margaret Thatcher has all the qualities of a poker – except for its occasional warmth.

Margaret Thatcher once gave a rousing speech in a little Yorkshire mining village. She was carried from the platform amid loud cheering by six local men.

'No need to carry me,' she shrieked, 'I can walk to the car.'

'Car nothing,' said the leader of the men gruffly, 'we're taking you to the canal.'

Margaret Thatcher was once asked by a newspaper reporter what her policy was towards black unemployed young people.

'I think that black unemployed young people,' she said, 'should be given a fair crack of the whip.'

A prominent Labour politician once described Margaret Thatcher as the only really masculine figure in the Conservative Party.

New theme song for the Conservative Party: *Maggie U-Turn Me On.*

What is the first reference to British Rail in the Bible?
'Then God created all creeping things.'

She was only a grocer's daughter but she taught Sir Geoffrey Howe.

Margaret Thatcher and the Chancellor of the Exchequer were walking down Oxford Street looking in the shop windows.
'I don't know why everyone is complaining about prices,' she said to him, 'look at that shop there – a sports jacket for £20, a pair of trousers for £10, that's pretty reasonable.'
'That is not a clothes shop, PM,' he corrected her, 'it's a dry cleaners.'

Margaret Thatcher, weeping bitterly, was standing at the edge of a cliff over which a busload of Trade Unionists had just plunged.

'At least you're showing some sympathy,' a reporter commented.

'Sympathy nothing,' she snorted, 'there were two empty seats on that bus.'

Ideally, Margaret Thatcher would prefer all countries except Britain to leave the Common Market.

Margaret Thatcher went into a shop and asked for a box of matches.

'Are you sure they are top quality matches, made by British workmen?' she asked the shopkeeper.

'Yes madam,' he replied proudly, 'I guarantee every one of them is a lightning striker.'

Margaret Thatcher has a new plan to end unemployment – raise the school-leaving age to fifty-seven.

Margaret Thatcher was having an audience with the Pope.

'And how is your good lady wife, Your Holiness?' she asked.

There was an embarrassed silence and an aide whispered to her, 'The Pope isn't allowed to have a wife.'

'All right, all right,' said Maggie irritably and loudly, 'How was I to know? Nobody is infallible.'

Margaret Thatcher and the Queen were driving to the State Opening of Parliament in the royal coach. Suddenly one of the horses broke wind very noisily.

'Oh, I do apologise,' said the highly embarrassed Monarch.

'That's all right, Your Majesty,' smiled Maggie sweetly, 'in fact I thought it was one of the horses.'

One of the things that Margaret Thatcher finds difficult to explain to young people is why a country that spends millions of pounds on Cruise missiles is trying to curb fireworks.

I f the great Samuel Johnson, cynic, lexicographer and wit had been asked about Margaret Thatcher he would probably have replied:

'A woman Prime Minister, sir, is like a dog walking on its hind legs; you don't expect it to be done well – the miracle is that it can be done at all.'

W hen Margaret Thatcher was an expectant mother she visited an ante-natal clinic and was informed that she was about to become the mother of twins.

'Impossible,' she shrieked, 'I demand a recount.' However, she immediately ordered Denis to apply for an increase in salary because he had increased his productivity by fifty per cent.

T here are only two things that Margaret Thatcher detests – racial discrimination and foreigners.

After all those years of marriage, Denis Thatcher is finally developing an attachment for his wife – it fits over her mouth.

What would we do if Maggie lost all her hair? Re-thatcher!

What are the four critical periods for unemployment under Margaret Thatcher's administration? Spring, summer, autumn and winter.

All the EEC prime ministers were in a boat on Lake Geneva when it hit a rock and sprung a leak.

'Thank heavens,' said Margaret Thatcher to herself, 'the leak is not at my end of the boat.'

What sort of present do you give the Cabinet Minister who has everything? Penicillin.

A Labour MP fell on hard times and died, but without a penny to his name. His colleagues were taking up a collection to give him a decent burial.

'Will you give us £10,' they asked Margaret Thatcher, 'to help bury a Labour MP?'

'Look,' said Maggie, 'here's £100. Bury ten of them!'

W hat do the letters PMT stand for?
Prime Minister Thatcher.

M argaret Thatcher claims that under her policies the people of Britain are becoming physically stronger. For example, ten years ago it took two fully grown people to carry £20-worth of groceries. Today a six-year-old child can do it.

T here is a lovely old British ritual concerning the opening of a session of the House of Commons that is still observed today. The Speaker of the House calls the members to order, looks at Margaret Thatcher and then prays for the country.

Margaret Thatcher has never quite got over the embarrassing fact that she was born while her mother was in labour.

One afternoon, while walking along a canal bank Margaret Thatcher happened to slip and fall in. Her screams for help were heard by a plucky young lad of fourteen who dived in, rescued her and brought her ashore.

'Name anything you desire,' she told him, 'and it shall be yours.'

'I'd like a state funeral,' said the young fellow.

'Why on earth do you want a funeral?' she asked in amazement.

'That's what I'm going to need,' said the young fellow, 'when my father finds out who I've rescued.'

Margaret Thatcher died and arrived at the gates of heaven. To nobody's surprise except her own, she was turned away and told to seek accommodation elsewhere. About an hour later, St Peter was roused by a loud knocking at his door. He went outside to find two hundred devils looking for political asylum.

We've all heard about the fellow who broke into the Queen's bedroom, but have you heard about the fellow who broke into Margaret Thatcher's bedroom?

He has a new career as a very promising soprano.

Margaret Thatcher worships her husband Denis like a god. She must do – she places a burnt offering before him every morning.

Times haven't changed very much since the reign of Queen Elizabeth I when an observer savagely described England as 'a dunghill on which the hens crow louder than the cocks'.

Margaret Thatcher speaking on unemployment – 'Things are going to get a lot worse before they get worse.'

Margaret Thatcher boasts that she is a self-made woman. That certainly relieves the Almighty of a dreadful responsibility.

In the election campaign Margaret Thatcher was canvassing one of her constituents.

'Vote for me,' she told him, 'and I promise you will never be unemployed again.'

'You're probably right,' he replied, 'I'm a gravedigger.'

Margaret Thatcher is one of the most fair-minded women on earth. She hates all foreigners equally, regardless of race, creed or colour.

Margaret Thatcher threw a big party at Number Ten and asked a celebrated international pianist of humble origins to provide the music. After some discussion they settled on a fee of £300 for the evening.

'Of course,' she reminded him haughtily, 'you are

not to mix with my guests or engage them in conversation.'

'In that case madam,' he replied with a gallant bow, 'my fee will be only £50.'

W hat is Maggie's pet name for Denis?
Pas de deux (father of twins).

M ark Thatcher was on the losing crew in a boat race and was being consoled by his mother.

'Never mind, darling,' she told him, 'it wasn't your fault. You rowed much faster than anyone else in your boat.'

M argaret and Denis were on holiday in Turkey and naturally were staying in the best hotel in town. One morning it was suggested by their guide that they return home at once as there was a strong possibility of an earthquake in the area.

'But surely,' smiled Maggie sweetly, 'those dreadful things only happen in working-class areas of the town?'

M argaret Thatcher's grasp of Central American affairs is not all it might be. For example, she thinks El Salvador is a Mexican bullfighter.

M argaret Thatcher was Guest of Honour at a provincial constituency dinner. The local MP scribbled her a note while she was at dinner, and as she had difficulty reading it she asked the man on her right to read it to her. He read – 'Please talk to the man on your right. I realise he's a terrible bore and a total idiot, but he's a big subscriber to party funds.'

W hen Margaret Thatcher was formulating her unemployment policy she took an evening off to go to a symphony concert. Next morning she made the following report:

(i) For long periods the five oboe players had nothing to do. Their number should be reduced and their work spread over the whole orchestra thus rationalising the situation.

(ii) All twelve violins were playing the same note. This is unnecessary duplication and the staff in this section should be cut by half. If a large volume of sound is really required, electronic amplification should be used.

(iii) Much effort was exerted in the playing of demisemiquavers. This is an unnecessary refinement and it is recommended that in future all notes should be rounded off to the nearest semiquaver. Then it should be possible to use trainees and unskilled operatives to play these notes, which would give rise to considerable savings.

(iv) No useful purpose is served by repeating with the horns passages already played by the strings. If such redundant passages were removed, the length of most pieces could be considerably shortened.

(v) Some of the violins are hundreds of years old, and foreign produced. Such obsolete equipment should be replaced with British-produced instruments for greater efficiency.

(vi) British music must become competitive!

Having watched Ipswich winning the Cup Final, Margaret Thatcher was asked to nominate her man of the match. She replied, 'Without a doubt, Whymark, number ten.' What her aides had neglected to point out was that while Whymark's name had been listed in the programme, he had not played because of injury!

Margaret Thatcher went to her doctor complaining of insomnia.

'No matter what I do,' she told him, 'I just can't seem to get to sleep at night.'

'Have you tried listening to a reading of one of your own speeches?' suggested the doctor.

Good news, bad news:
Good news – Margaret Thatcher has resigned as Prime Minister.
Bad news – It's not true.

An Australian, a Frenchman and an Englishman were boasting about progress in their respective countries.

'There was a bloke in Melbourne,' said the Australian, 'who lost a leg, and one of our surgeons gave him a transplant and a month later he was looking for work.'

'In our country,' said the Frenchman, 'a man had a new heart put in and within two weeks he was looking for work.'

'I can top that,' said the Englishman, 'we put a woman into Number Ten and now there are three million people looking for work.'

Margaret Thatcher was out walking one afternoon when she came across three little boys with a dog in a large cardboard box.

'What's going on?' she asked them.

'Well', said one of the lads, 'we're having a competition to see who can tell the biggest lie, and the winner gets this dog.'

'That's shocking,' said Margaret Thatcher, 'I'm glad to say I've never told a lie in my life.'

'Give the lady the dog, Alf,' said one boy to the others.

Margaret Thatcher reports that this has been an average year for unemployment. That means it is a good deal worse than last year and a good deal better than next year.

Among the graffiti on the wall of a Japanese-owned car factory in the British Midlands was seen the following tribute to Margaret Thatcher's policies:
Buy Blitish.

Let's look on the bright side of Margaret Thatcher's policies for a change. Some of her policies have led to thousands of jobs being created – mostly for receivers, though.

An Irishman was standing outside the House of Commons shouting at the top of his voice, 'Mrs Thatcher is a dangerous fool who is ruining the country!' He was arrested, charged and convicted and given two sentences. The first was a three-month suspended sentence for disturbing the peace. The second sentence was three years hard labour for giving away state secrets.

A very left-wing English newspaper printed an article in which it was stated that half of Margaret Thatcher's cabinet were gangsters. Furiously, she phoned the editor and demanded that the newspaper publish an immediate retraction. Next day, the newspaper apologised and stated that half of Margaret Thatcher's cabinet were not gangsters.

At least nobody can accuse Margaret Thatcher of being two-faced. If she was, she would hardly be wearing the face she's got on now.

Margaret Thatcher once dreamed she was giving a speech in the House of Commons, and woke up to find she was.

Newsflash: Margaret Thatcher, while driving on the M1, has just been in collision with an articulated lorry. She was stated to be unharmed but the lorry is not expected to recover.

Margaret Thatcher has asked people to vote for the Conservative Party and sound economic policies. Doesn't she know it's illegal to vote twice?

According to a well-known Labour politician, being attacked by Geoffrey Howe is like being savaged by a dead sheep.

Some idea of the problems facing Britain's unemployed can be gauged from the fact that Margaret Thatcher thinks that manual labour is a Spanish trade union official.

According to some reports, Margaret Thatcher started life as a raw inexperienced dishwasher in a London café. However, she never lived up to this early promise.

Margaret Thatcher was stopped in the street by a tramp who asked her for twenty pence for a cup of coffee.
'Show me the cup of coffee first,' she said.

Margaret Thatcher was describing her travels in the Far East: 'We went riding in one of those rickshaws,' she told a friend, 'and believe it or not, they have horses that look just like men.'

An airliner containing the EEC Prime Ministers was in difficulty over Europe and the captain announced that they were losing altitude rapidly. He suggested that to save the plane one of them would have to jump out.

'I do this for the glory of Germany,' said the German Prime Minster, and jumped out.

'We need to lose more weight,' said the captain, so the French Prime Minister shouted, 'I do this for the glory of France,' and jumped out.

'Sorry,' said the captain, 'I'm afraid we need to lose the weight of just one more person.'

'I do this for the glory of England,' said Margaret Thatcher with great dignity, and threw out the Irish Prime Minister.

Margaret Thatcher died and knocked on the gates of heaven. To her surprise the gates were opened not by St Peter, but by a devil.

'Don't be surprised,' said the devil, 'we've gone comprehensive.'

Margaret Thatcher just cannot understand the continuing strife in the Middle East. She thinks that the Arabs and the Jews should learn to live in peace like all good Christians.

A little boy asked his father, an ardent Trade Unionist, what was the difference between a disaster and a catastrophe.

'My son,' he told him, 'if Margaret Thatcher fell into the Thames that would be a disaster; if someone pulled her out again, *that* would be a catastrophe.'

An extract from one of Margaret Thatcher's political speeches: 'If you vote for our opponents, you will get a pig in a poke; vote for me and get the real thing. Our opponents in the Labour Party have been lying in government for years; now *we* want a chance.'

Margaret Thatcher's birthday was coming up and Denis couldn't decide what to buy her. He decided to take the bull by the horns and ask her.

'What would you like for your birthday, my little petal?' he asked her.

'Nothing in particular,' she replied, 'but whatever it is, if you can afford it, forget about it.'

Margaret Thatcher has the highest possible regard for the truth; so much so that she uses it only on very special occasions.

A starving trade unionist had walked from Glasgow to present a petition to Margaret Thatcher in her country residence. To make his point, he went down on all fours on her lawn and began to eat the grass.

'What on earth are you up to?' she asked from her study window.

'My family and I are starving,' he replied, 'and I can find nothing to eat except this grass.'

'My dear fellow,' she smiled sweetly, 'why not come round to the back lawn? The grass is much longer there.'

Over the automatic hand-dryer at Trade Union headquarters someone had written:
PRESS THIS BUTTON FOR A ONE MINUTE SPEECH FROM MRS THATCHER.

The Conservatives once fought a by-election in a constituency with a large immigrant population, many of whom were unemployed. Margaret Thatcher gave the following reason for the fact that her party was so heavily defeated:

'Many of these people think that the Labour Exchange, on which they depend so much, actually belongs to the Labour Party and that we would close it if we won the by-election.'

Margaret Thatcher's idea of politics is based on getting votes from the poor and party funds from the rich by promising to protect each from the other.

For Christmas, Margaret Thatcher bought Denis two beautiful hats, one yellow and one green. On Christmas morning he came down to breakfast proudly wearing his yellow hat.

'What's the matter with the green one then?' she said haughtily.

Margaret Thatcher was on her deathbed and her loyal cabinet was debating what kind of gravestone they would put over her grave. Finally, out of force of habit, they decided to consult her.

'Would you like a granite headstone or a marble one?' they asked.

'No need for anything like that,' she droned, 'after all, it's only going to be for three days.'

Margaret Thatcher's name is now a household word throughout the world, but remember that rubbish is also a household word.

Margaret Thatcher was window shopping one afternoon with her bodyguard, a plainclothes policeman. They saw some silver napkin rings in a jeweller's window so she asked her bodyguard what they were.

'They are napkin rings, madam,' he replied.

'And what are they used for?' she persisted.

'Well, some people cannot afford freshly laundered linen napkins at every meal, so they roll their napkins up after every meal, and put them in those rings.'

'Oh my God,' said Margaret Thatcher, 'can such poverty exist?'

Denis Thatcher was reading *The Times* and became very excited when he saw that some of his shares had made a huge gain on the stock market. He rushed into the bathroom where his wife was having a bath and shouted, 'My God, look at these share prices.'

'How many times must I tell you Denis,' she smiled at him, 'that when nobody else is present you may call me Margaret.'

Independent Television once announced the following programme change:

Southern Television, Sunday July 4th – 4.40: The Big Film. Delete 'The Prime Minister' and substitute 'The Rat'.

Seen scrawled on a wall:
GET MAGGIE THATCHER BEFORE SHE GETS ... AAAAAAH.

Margaret Thatcher's government taxes the places that other governments can't reach.

One of Margaret Thatcher's constituents once called on her to ask a favour.

'Let's play a little game,' she told him. 'Actually, I've got a glass eye and if you can guess which one it is, I'll let you have your request.'

The man looked at her carefully and said finally, 'It's the left one.'

'You're correct,' she replied, 'but how on earth did you guess? Nine out of ten people guess wrongly.'

'I thought the left one had a good deal more warmth and humanity than the right one,' replied the man.

Margaret Thatcher was attending a cocktail party and was in conversation with a young man anxious to impress her.

'When can we look forward to reading your memoirs, Mrs Thatcher?' he asked her.

'I shall probably publish my memoirs posthumously,' she replied.

'Oh how super,' he enthused, 'I do hope it will be soon.'

Margaret Thatcher denies vehemently that she is a rich woman. However, she does concede that her husband Denis is a rich man.

The question that all Maggie's opponents are asking is this: Where is Guy Fawkes now when his country really needs him?

To all those people who argue that at the back of it all Margaret Thatcher is really a nice woman there can be only one reply. My mother is a really nice woman too, but I don't think she should be prime minister!

Some of the men Margaret Thatcher has appointed to run British Steel will never see a blast furnace until after they are dead.

'We have, of course, often done it before, but never on a pavement outside a hotel in Eastbourne. We have done it in various rooms in one way or another at various functions. It is perfectly genuine and normal – and normal and right – so to do.'
– William Whitelaw on kissing Margaret Thatcher

Actually, Margaret Thatcher is quite a modest woman. But then she has such a lot to be modest about.

Margaret Thatcher was talking to a man at a party and couldn't for the life of her remember who he was or where she had met him before. Desperately, she kicked for touch.

'Still in the same job, are you?' she smiled.

'Yes I am, actually,' said the man rather sourly.

'And your father,' she continued, 'is he well?'

'Very well, thank you.'

'And your mother,' she asked in desperation, 'is she well?'

'Yes,' said the man, 'she is very well too, and still Queen.'

Actually, on a purely personal basis, nobody likes Margaret Thatcher more than the leader of the Labour Party – and he detests her.

Margaret Thatcher was on an official visit to Hong Kong and was being taken on a conducted tour. The party passed by an open public swimming pool in which over a dozen men were swimming in the nude. She ordered her car to stop and asked her guide if it was not considered indecent for people to behave thus in public.

'No, honourable lady,' replied the guide. 'In this country we only consider it indecent for people to stop and watch them.'

'Mrs Thatcher has one great disadvantage – she is a daughter of the people and looks neat and trim as daughters of the people desire to be. Shirley Williams on the other hand has such an advantage over her because she is a member of the upper middle classes and can achieve that distraught kitchen sink revolting look that one cannot acquire unless one has been to a really good school.'

– Rebecca West

Margaret Thatcher was visiting a psychiatric hospital and decided to introduce herself to some of the patients.

'How do you do,' she said to one old man, 'I'm Margaret Thatcher, the Prime Minister.'

'Don't worry,' said the old man, 'they will soon cure you of that. When I came here I thought I was Harold Wilson.'

Denis Thatcher was shopping at his local butcher's. He saw some steak that looked particularly nice, so he asked the assistant, 'Is that steak tender?'

'It's as tender as your wife's heart, sir,' said the butcher.

'Perhaps I'll have the lamb chops,' said Denis.

Motto for Margaret Thatcher – Happiness can't buy you money.

Margaret Thatcher realises that she doesn't have to fool all the people all of the time. She just has to fool a majority of them at election time.

Rumours of a split in Margaret Thatcher's cabinet have been greatly exaggerated. Why, during her recent illness they wished her 'get well soon' by ten votes to nine, with only four abstentions.

Winston Churchill was once asked what were the qualifications essential for a politician. He gave the following reply:

'A politician must have the ability to foretell what will happen tomorrow, what will happen next month and what will happen next year – and also the ability to explain afterwards why it didn't happen.'

How on earth did he know all about Margaret Thatcher?

British comedians nowadays don't need to make jokes – they merely observe Margaret Thatcher's government and report the facts.

Two West Country farmers were watching Margaret Thatcher giving a party political broadcast on television. After some time one of them remarked: 'I think she uses all those fancy words because she's afraid that if us common people knew what she was talking about, then we would know that she didn't know what she was talking about.'

When Margaret Thatcher was first chosen to stand as Conservative candidate, she rushed home excitedly to tell Denis.

'Denis, Denis, I've been selected,' she panted.

'Honestly?' yawned Denis.

'Now why on earth did you have to bring that up?' she scowled.

'When I tell the folks back home that the Poms have got a sheila as a prime minister, they go hysterical.'

— Australian comedian Paul Hogan

Margaret Thatcher claims in all sincerity that she hasn't got an enemy in the world. Maybe so – but none of her friends like her.

Margaret Thatcher was seriously ill and Denis was called to her hospital bedside.

'Well, Denis,' she said to him feebly, 'it looks as if I shan't be a nuisance to you much longer.'

'That's nonsense dear,' said the ever-tactful Denis, 'of course you will.'

According to Margaret Thatcher's political enemies, the only Tory that is good for anything is a lavatory.

Even as a baby Margaret Thatcher showed that she had the makings of a perfect politician. Her parents relate that at the age of nine months she could make more noises that sounded well and meant nothing than any other child in the country.

It was a merciful decision of providence to allow Margaret and Denis Thatcher to marry each other and so make only two people miserable instead of four.

A hanger-on once tried to impress Margaret Thatcher by suggesting that she and Winston Churchill were the only two great politicians of the twentieth century.
'Why drag in Churchill?' she retorted.

Margaret Thatcher went to her physician for a check-up. After he had given her a thorough examination he told her, 'You're as sound as a pound.'
'My God,' she gasped, 'am I as bad as that?'

Most people wish they were as sure about any-thing as Margaret Thatcher seems to be about everything.

Two Irishmen arrived on Margaret Thatcher's doorstep and offered to dig the Channel Tunnel for £500.

'How do you plan to do it?' she asked them.

'Well,' said one of the Irishmen, 'to speed up operations, I'll start to dig on the French side, while my colleague here with the large shovel will start to dig on the English side.'

'But,' she protested, 'what happens if there is even a slight error in your calculations and the pair of you fail to meet?'

'Then,' smiled the Irishman, 'you get two Channel Tunnels for the price of one.'

Margaret Thatcher was once offered a million dollars to appear as the centrefold of *Playboy* magazine with her vital organ uncovered – her mouth.

A travelling salesman arrived up at a hotel one night and asked for a room.

'I'm terribly sorry,' said the clerk, 'all our rooms are full.'

'But you must have something left,' said the salesman.

'No,' said the clerk, 'not a thing I'm afraid.'

'Look,' said the salesman, 'If Mrs Thatcher arrived up at the moment, could you fit her in?'

'Well, I think we might manage that,' smiled the clerk.

'Look,' said the salesman, 'Maggie can't make it – so I'll have her room.'

Margaret Thatcher once gave a speech to the inmates of a psychiatric hospital. However, she was continually interrupted by one man with shouts of 'rubbish', 'garbage' and 'that's a load of old cobblers'.

After the speech she turned furiously to the chief medical officer and asked him if he was going to reprimand the man in question.

'On the contrary', beamed the doctor, 'that man has been a patient here for the last twenty years and this is the first sign of improvement we've seen in him.'

Margaret Thatcher's Northern Ireland policy can be summed up in one sentence: 'Let us not prejudge the past.'

In Margaret Thatcher's constituency, a canvasser was doing a door-to-door survey to discern peoples' voting intentions. He called at one door and asked the man who opened it what he thought of Margaret Thatcher.

The man replied, 'She is an unscrupulous scoundrel completely devoid of intellect, decency and integrity, and an infamous bandit whose sole aim in life is to feather her nest with ill-gotten gains taken from the starving working classes.'

'Thank you,' said the canvasser and marked 'doubtful' on his list.

Margaret Thatcher had been giving the same boring policy speeches to her cabinet for over five years so she decided to have them recorded and played to the cabinet instead. One day she happened to look in on the room where meetings took place to see how the scheme was working out. She found a room empty of people with her tape recorder talking merrily away to over a dozen other tape recorders.

It's true – jumble up the letters of the words MAGGIE THATCHER and you get THAT GRIM EEC HAG.

Margaret Thatcher's favourite newspaper headline: DENSE FOG IN THE CHANNEL CONTINENT COMPLETELY CUT OFF

Something Sydney Smith, the great nineteenth-century English wit, once said, seems to fit Margaret and Denis Thatcher so perfectly:
 'I like them. I like him; he's so lady-like. And I like her; she's always such a perfect gentleman.'

Margaret Thatcher was once introducing Norman St John Stevas to the Pope.
 'Your Holiness,' she intoned, 'I'd like you to meet Norman St John Stevas, who, like Your Holiness, is a Roman Catholic.'

Denis Thatcher once gave up gin for a week. However, he soon went back again because he didn't want to become a slave to self-control.

Margaret Thatcher was speaking at a political meeting in Glasgow: 'I was born an English Conservative,' she thundered, 'I have lived all my life as an English Conservative, and I hope to die an English Conservative.'

'Have you no ambition, woman?' came a voice from the audience.

'No woman in my time will be Prime Minister. Anyway I wouldn't want to be Prime Minister ...'

– Margaret Thatcher in 1969.

Margaret Thatcher was visiting a wounded soldier in hospital in Northern Ireland.

'And where have you been injured, my good man?' she asked him.

'In the Falls, madam,' he replied.

'No,' she persisted, 'what part of your body was injured?'

'Let me put it this way,' said the soldier, 'if you had been injured where I was injured, you wouldn't have been injured at all.'

Margaret Thatcher once confided to a newspaper reporter: 'I haven't had a proper holiday since 1971.'

'But,' he protested, 'you've only just returned from a three week vacation in Switzerland.'

'I know,' she sighed, 'but Denis was with me.'

In a fit of wild enthusiasm Margaret Thatcher decided to tell Denis an Irishman joke.

'It's about two Irishmen,' she told him, 'one of whom sold the other two skulls, one of Queen Victoria as a girl and the other of Queen Victoria as an old woman.'

'That sounds like a very funny one,' said Denis, 'How does it go?'

A Tory MP died and was carried to the great hereafter. To everybody's amazement he said, 'This is an absolutely fantastic place – I'll even go so far as to say that not even life in England is as good as life in Heaven.'

'But,' they told him, 'this isn't Heaven.'

What is the best thing you can get out of Margaret Thatcher's Britain?

A jumbo jet to Tokyo.

The German Prime Minister, the French Prime Minister and Margaret Thatcher were stranded in a little boat together. A little island appeared a short distance away so the German Prime Minister walked across the water to it and returned with some food. Margaret Thatcher walked across the water and returned with some coconut milk to drink. The French Prime Minister left the boat, started out for the island but disappeared from sight under the water.

'Do you think we should have told him where the stepping stones were?' smiled the German Prime Minister.

'What stepping stones?' said Margaret Thatcher coldly.

Sticker seen on the back of a car in London: *Warning – Mark Thatcher taught me to drive this car.*

Margaret Thatcher and Denis were having breakfast together. He was hiding behind his newspaper and she was nattering on and on about inflation and the laziness of the working classes. Suddenly she turned on him angrily and said, 'Denis, I do wish you would pay a little attention to me when I'm talking about important policy matters.'

'I'm paying you as little attention as I can, dear,' mumbled Denis, reaching for another piece of toast.

'For the purposes of government a country of 55 million people is forced to depend on the pooled talent of a cabinet which could not sustain a single multinational company.'

– Sir John Hoskyns.

Denis Thatcher was once asked by a newspaper reporter what his favourite breakfast was.

'It consists,' he replied, 'of a pound of well done steak, a bottle of Scotch whisky and a large alsatian dog.'

'What on earth is the dog for?' asked the mystified reporter.

'To eat the steak of course,' smiled Denis.

An Irishman was charged with assaulting Margaret Thatcher and was asked to stand in an identification parade. As Margaret Thatcher came in to inspect the parade the Irishman shouted, 'That's her, that's her, I'd recognise that face anywhere!'

An enterprising firm has just put a bionic version of Denis Thatcher on the market. It costs £5.

Which of the following is odd man out?
Donald Duck, The Archbishop of Canterbury, King Kong, an intellectual in Margaret Thatcher's cabinet and Popeye?

The Archbishop of Canterbury – all the others are purely fictitious characters.

Margaret Thatcher was on an election tour talking to the people. One man informed her that he had just lost his job.

'For what reason?' she asked him.

'No reason,' he replied, 'I was just made redundant.'

'Thank heavens for that,' she smiled, 'just think how awful it would have been for you and your family if you had been dismissed in disgrace.'

Before she became a politician, Margaret Thatcher trained as a chemist. Nowadays she thinks copper nitrate is overtime money paid to policemen.

Description of Margaret Thatcher by an Irish politician – she has a face like a well-kept grave.

Margaret Thatcher suggested that Willie Whitelaw seek political asylum – in the House of Lords!

Margaret Thatcher once gave a reception for the England football team because they had won the toss in a recent match. She was asked to pose for the press with a football in each hand. Next day the newspaper caption on the photograph ran:

At Long Last Maggie Has Got Her Hands Where She Wants Them – On The Strikers' *****!

'If the Good Lord had intended us to have equal rights to go out and work he wouldn't have created men and women.'
– One of Margaret Thatcher's ministers in 1980.

Margaret Thatcher feels that every time she produces an answer to the Irish Question the Irish change the question.

Contrary to what is widely believed, Margaret Thatcher really does want equal pay for women. However, she intends to achieve it by lowering mens' wages to the level of womens'!

Isn't it funny how Margaret Thatcher is the British Prime Minister, yet the only people who really know how to run the country seem to be taxi drivers, barbers and barmen?

What would Denis Thatcher do if he found his wife with another man?
He'd grab the man's white stick and hit him over the head with it.

An Irishman got a job as a chauffeur to Margaret Thatcher and gave every satisfaction as a driver. However, she noticed that he was a little careless about his personal appearance and in particular that he didn't seem to shave every day, so she decided to drop a few discreet hints.

'Paddy,' she said casually one morning to him, 'How often do you think one should shave?'

'Well ma'am,' he replied slowly, 'with a light growth like yours, I'd say about once every three days.'

Denis Thatcher isn't really into the drug scene. He once tried sniffing coke but the bubbles kept going up his nose.

A newspaper reporter once put the following question to Margaret Thatcher: 'Why don't world leaders realise that the countries of the world can solve all their problems if they decide to live in peace together?'

Margaret Thatcher replied, 'God forbid. The arms trade would collapse.'

How does Margaret Thatcher like the English climate? It doesn't disagree with her – it wouldn't dare to!

According to a well-known political commentator, Margaret Thatcher is the finest woman prime minister since Neville Chamberlain.

If Margaret Thatcher were to be knocked down by a bus, who would be elected the new prime minister? The bus driver!

The following is a description of Downing Street in a guide book to London:
Today the old-time hoodlums and robbers have vanished. The Prime Minister and the Chancellor of the Exchequer live there now.

Margaret Thatcher and Denis were marooned on a raft at sea and things looked very bleak indeed. After several days without food and water, she began to pray: 'Dear Lord, if you rescue us, I promise that I will change my ways. I will be kind to miners and the trade unions; I will not sack my ministers for trivial transgressions; I'll even visit Russia on a goodwill mission ...'

'Hang on a moment,' said Denis, 'don't get carried away. I think I can see a boat.'

Margaret Thatcher was on an election walkabout when she was stopped by a down-and-out who asked for some money.

'How dare you beg money from me in the street,' she said to him acidly.

'What do you expect me to do,' said the man, 'Open an office?'

Margaret Thatcher once took up ballooning as a hobby but it didn't work out. She couldn't get inflation to rise!

What do you call a statue of Margaret Thatcher? The immaculate misconception!

Margaret Thatcher boasts that British-made cars are getting better and better all the time. Take for example the matter of petrol tanks. Ten years ago the petrol tank of a British-made car could hold only £5 worth of petrol. Now it can hold £20 worth.

A certain Tory supporter who had contributed vast sums of money to the Conservative Party, continually pestered Margaret Thatcher with demands for a title. Alarmed by his uncouth behaviour, she refused, but gave him the next best thing. She allowed him to tell everyone that she had offered him a title but that he had refused to accept it.

Margaret Thatcher's private plane caught fire so she bailed out at thirty thousand feet and counted up to ten. Then she pulled the ripcord of her parachute but nothing happened. So she counted to ten again and pulled the emergency cord of the parachute, but again nothing happened. So she counted to ten a third time and pulled the fail-safe emergency cord, never known to fail, but yet again nothing happened.

'This is it,' she said to herself as she plummeted towards the earth, 'no fifth term in office for me.'

Then she cheered up because down below on earth she saw a dozen young Englishmen, all in the flower of their manhood, with arms outstretched, waiting to catch her. So she relaxed as she hurtled towards the ground.

Then she realised to her horror that they were members of the England cricket team.

A political commentator once remarked that putting Margaret Thatcher in charge of the National Health Service was a bit like putting King Herod on the board of Mothercare.

In a wild fit of extravagance, Margaret Thatcher invited her entire cabinet out to dinner in an expensive restaurant.

'And what would you like to have for the main course, madam?' asked the waiter.

'Steak,' she replied.

'And how about the vegetables, madam?'

'They'll have steak too,' she answered with a wave of the hand.

This is said to be Margaret Thatcher's favourite joke:

Doctor to patient – 'Are you on the National Health or would you like an anaesthetic?'

Sitting on Eastbourne beach was a man in a deckchair shouting, 'No, no, no, no, no, no, a thousand times No!'

Local people were very worried so they called in the police but they couldn't get any sense out of the fellow. Finally, a psychiatrist was called in and after a brief examination he assured them that there was no cause for concern. The man was one of Margaret Thatcher's yes-men on holiday.

The oldest man in Britain has just died. He can remember when the unemployment figure stood at two million.

A man was in despair because he owed £100 but had no way of getting the money in time, so he wrote and posted a letter to God asking him for the money. The post office were at a loss where to send the letter so they had a brainwave and sent it to Margaret Thatcher as the closest approximation to God that they could think of.

The letter came up at a cabinet meeting and Margaret Thatcher was so touched that she passed the hat around among her ministers. The collection came to £80 which they forwarded to the man, signing it, 'From God (via Tory Party Headquarters)'.

The overjoyed man received the money and immediately wrote the following letter of thanks:
'Dear God,
Thank you for the money that I have just received. But next time send it directly because those thieving bastards at Tory Party Headquarters stole £20.'

News item: Mrs Thatcher has just left on a world tour visiting all countries friendly to Britain. She is due back tomorrow.

Definition of the word 'unnecessary' – it's as unnecessary as Margaret Thatcher taking an assertiveness course.

A close friend of Margaret Thatcher is on record as saying that beneath that cold and forbidding exterior there beats an equally cold and forbidding heart.

There was a dinner party at Number Ten and Denis Thatcher was discussing the Middle East situation over a pre-dinner drink with a bishop.

'Well,' said the bishop, 'At least there is One Above who understands all, who knows all and who in time will solve all.'

'Yes,' said Denis, 'and she will be down in a moment.'

In which month do Tory ministers have the fewest sex scandals?
February.

Mrs Thatcher strongly recommends to all her fellow housewives a new radioactive washing powder that has come on the market. She says it's a nuclear detergent.

A Conservative MP was being shown around a factory where a great variety of unusual items were being made. One particular line of products greatly puzzled him because it seemed to resemble a part of a horse, so he asked the supervisor what it was.

'It's the front part of a horse,' said the supervisor, 'and when we have made them we send them to Tory Party Headquarters for final assembly.'

Margaret Thatcher was addressing a group of trade unionists about what life would ultimately be like for workers under her administration.

'We can guarantee you double wages,' she droned, 'nine months holidays every year, a four-hour lunch break and you will have to work only on Wednesdays.'

A shop steward's voice from the back interrupted her: 'What, every bloody Wednesday?'

Many, many years ago an old doctor was called out of bed at 4 a.m. to assist a woman in labour. He trudged through the snow and rain and arrived at the house well in time to assist at the long and difficult birth. Then he returned home to grab a few hours sleep before his surgery began, and as he tumbled into bed his wife remarked: 'Who would be a doctor? Is it ever worth all you have to go through?'

Before the old man nodded off to sleep he said to his wife, 'There are moments in my career that make it worth-while – guess who was born this morning – Margaret Thatcher.'

The secret of Margaret Thatcher's success is that she is the first politician to have mastered the art of faking sincerity.

Margaret Thatcher was asked in a radio interview what she would do in a totally hopeless situation.

She replied, 'This is neither the time nor the place to discuss the unemployment figures.'

Why is Cecil Parkinson like a piece of self-assembly furniture?
One screw in the wrong place and the entire cabinet falls apart.

Margaret Thatcher was canvassing in a London pub. Seated at the bar were three men.

'I will buy a drink,' she said, 'for whoever of the three of you gives me the best reason for voting for my party.'

'I'll vote Tory,' said the first, 'because of the economic prosperity under your rule.'

'I'll vote Tory,' said the second, 'because I hate the Labour Party.'

'And I'll vote Tory,' said the third, 'because I want that drink!'

Margaret Thatcher's cabinet are not renowned for their physical beauty. In fact they look as if somebody went berserk in a wax museum with a blow-torch.

Three men were being interviewed by Margaret Thatcher for the post of Party Information Officer. Each was asked the question, 'What is two plus two?' The first candidate answered, 'Four'. He didn't get the job because she felt he was too blunt and tactless.

The next candidate answered, 'Usually four.' He didn't get the job because she felt he was too indecisive.

It was the third candidate who got the job. He answered her, 'What would you like it to be?'

The political correspondent of *The Times* wandered into the editor's office.

'What did Mrs Thatcher have to say in her speech last night?' asked the editor.

'Absolutely nothing, as usual,' said the correspondent.

'Keep it down to two columns then,' said the editor.

'Margaret Thatcher sounds like the *Book of Revelations* read out over a railway station public address system by a headmistress of uncertain age wearing calico knickers.'

– Clive James.

Cecil Parkinson was at home in bed with his wife when there was a sudden thunderstorm. As a great flash of lightning lit up the room Cecil jumped out of bed shouting, 'I'll buy the negatives, I'll buy the negatives!'

A burglar broke into Margaret Thatcher's bedroom but all he took was one look.

D enis Thatcher was having a bath at Number Ten one morning when his wife suddenly burst into the bathroom unannounced. Denis hastily groped for a towel to cover himself up.

'Now, now, Denis,' she laughed, 'there's no need to be so coy; after all we've been married for a long time.'

'It's not that,' mumbled Denis, 'it's just that any time you see something big you want to privatise it.'

W hat do the letters SDP stand for?
Support David Please.

W hy is Margaret Thatcher unpopular even in Warsaw?
Because of the Poll Tax.

During a heated Parliamentary debate a member of the Opposition rose and asked the Speaker if it was in order to call Margaret Thatcher a sewer rat.

'Certainly not,' said the Speaker, 'That would be completely out of order.'

'In that case,' smiled the MP, 'the sewer rats will be pleased.'

Margaret Thatcher was asked if she had heard the latest political jokes.

'Heard them?' she retorted, 'I've appointed them all.'

It is said that if Margaret Thatcher had been present at the creation of the universe she would have given the Almighty some very useful hints.

What is the difference between Margaret Thatcher and a banana?
Some people like bananas.

What is the definition of collective responsibility? Margaret Thatcher makes a decision and the entire cabinet agrees with it.

How can you tell if Margaret Thatcher is lying? Her lips are moving.

What are Margaret Thatcher's favourite comedy programmes on television?
SDLP, SDP and Labour Party political broadcasts.

Neil Kinnock was holding forth about his political principles at a public meeting.
'I'd rather be right than prime minister any day,' he told his audience.
'Don't worry,' shouted a heckler, 'you're never likely to be either.'

Margaret Thatcher is getting her own television series. It's going to be called 'Plunder Woman'.

The difference between Margaret Thatcher and Neil Kinnock is the difference between bacon and eggs. For the pig, bacon represents total commitment while for the hen an egg represents only partial involvement.

Have you heard the one about the MP who is leaving politics and joining the SDLP?

It is said that every one of Margaret Thatcher's ministers carries a little card saying: 'I am a government minister. In case of accident call a press conference.'

Have you heard the one about the Tory supporter who joined the Democrats? He raised the level of intelligence in both parties.

Economic realists in the party are not fooled by Margaret Thatcher's claims that there is light at the end of the tunnel. They feel it's just the light of an oncoming train.

What's the difference between Margaret Thatcher's full employment for all policy and Santa Claus?
There is a remote possibility that there is a Santa Claus.

It is not widely known that Margaret Thatcher is noted for her financial generosity to the Trade Union movement. She gives the unions large cheques, but, because she likes to remain anonymous, she never signs them.

After losing his deposit in the by-election an SDLP candidate complained to the media that he was a victim.

'A victim of what?' asked a reporter.

'A victim of accurate counting' replied the SDLP candidate.

An enthusiastic SDLP candidate stood for election and lost his deposit, receiving only a handful of votes for his trouble. A few days later he was picked up by the police and was charged with carrying a handgun without a permit.

'Do you have any excuse to offer?' the judge asked him.

'Look,' he replied, 'a man with as few friends as I've got in this constituency needs all the protection he can get.'

'Case dismissed,' said the judge.

An election poster read: The SDLP are the answer!

Underneath someone had written: 'It must have been a pretty silly question!'

Maggie Hits Back

Margaret Thatcher was speaking at a political meeting where she was continually heckled by a particularly spotty left-wing youth.

'Don't you wish you were a man?' he shouted at her.

'No,' she replied, 'but don't you?'

Margaret Thatcher once suggested to the Labour Party that they should nationalise crime. Then they could be sure it would never pay.

Actually, Margaret Thatcher thinks the world of the SDLP. And like the world, she would like to see it flattened at the polls.

Margaret Thatcher was addressing a meeting in a rural area and facing a rather hostile crowd. Suddenly, a large cabbage was thrown at her, narrowly missing her ear. Without turning a hair she quipped, 'I see one of my opponents has lost his head.'

Margaret Thatcher once put down a political opponent with the following words: 'The honourable member is indebted to his memory for his jests and his imagination for his facts.'

The Liberal Party, according to Margaret Thatcher, is merely a convenient device whereby disgruntled Conservative voters can register a mild protest against their own party without giving any advantage to the Labour Party.

Margaret Thatcher is not above the odd superior remark. When asked what she thought of the Emperor Haile Selasse she said, 'He was one of the nicest emperors I have ever met!'

Margaret Thatcher was giving a public lecture when she was heckled by a voice from the seated audience objecting to what she said.

'Stand up, sir,' she retorted, whereupon a tiny little man from the audience stood up.

'Sit down, now, sir,' said Margaret Thatcher. 'The insignificance of your appearance is sufficient to answer the impudence of your objection.'

Margaret Thatcher claims that the Labour Party wants to form a special trade union for people who don't wish to belong to a trade union.

Margaret Thatcher has a quaint definition of the most recent Labour Party manifesto: the longest suicide note ever written.

Margaret Thatcher tells the following story to illustrate Labour Party policy:

A workman was asked to dispose of some rubble so he suggested digging a large hole to put it in.

'What will you do with the contents of the hole?' he was asked.

'I'll dig another hole,' said the workman.

'But how do you know it will all fit in the second hole?' persisted his boss.

'I'll dig the other hole deeper,' said the workman.

Margaret Thatcher's description of the Liberal Party: A party that looks neither to the left nor the right but continues to drive straight down the middle of the road.

In her early political days Margaret Thatcher was canvassing in a country village where the little hall proved too small to hold her audience. As it was a fine day they moved outdoors but then another problem arose – there was no platform from which she could speak. Finally a local farmer offered a manure spreader for her to stand on – amid guffaws from the crowd. But she was equal to the task.

'Ladies and gentlemen,' she opened her speech, 'This is the first time I have ever spoken from a Labour platform.'

Great Humour Titles from Angus & Robertson:

☐ The World's Best Dirty Jokes	Mr J	£2.50
☐ More of the World's Best Dirty Jokes	Mr J	£2.50
☐ Still More of the World's Best Dirty Jokes	Mr J	£2.50
☐ The World's Best Irish Jokes	Mr O'S	£2.50
☐ More of the World's Best Irish Jokes	Mr O'S	£2.50
☐ The World's Best Jewish Jokes	Ben Eliezer	£2.50
☐ More of The World's Best Jewish Jokes	Ben Eliezer	£1.99
☐ The World's Best Doctor Jokes	Dr Raja Korale	£2.50
☐ The World's Best Dirty Stories	John Gurney	£2.50
☐ The World's Best Dirty Limericks		£2.50
☐ The World's Best Mother-in-Law Jokes	Des MacHale	£2.50
☐ The World's Best Fishing Jokes	John Gurney	£2.50
☐ The World's Best Salesman Jokes	John Gurney	£2.50
☐ The World's Best Scottish Jokes	Des MacHale	£2.50
☐ The World's Best Golf Jokes	Robert McCune	£2.99
☐ The World's Best Cricket Jokes	Ernest Forbes	£2.99
☐ The World's Best Maggie Thatcher Jokes	Des MacHale	£2.99
☐ The World's Best Lawyer Jokes	Edward Phillips	£2.99
☑ The World's Best Business Jokes	Charles Alverson	£2.50
☐ The World's Best Holiday Jokes	Edward Phillips	£2.50
☐ The World's Best Acting Jokes		£2.50
☐ The Complete Wit and Wisdom of the Irish	Des MacHale	£2.95
☐ No Worries: How to Survive Australians	Robert Treborlang	£2.95
☐ G'Day! Teach Yourself Australian	Colin Bowles	£3.50

ANGUS & ROBERTSON (UK) BOOKSERVICE BY POST, PO BOX 29, DOUGLAS, ISLE OF MAN, BRITISH ISLES

NAME ....

ADDRESS ....

....

....

Please enclose a cheque or postal order made out to Angus & Robertson (UK) for the amount due and allow the following for postage and packing.
UK CUSTOMERS: Please allow 22p per book to a maximum of £3.00.
B.F.P.O. & EIRE: Please allow 22p per book to a maximum of £3.00.
OVERSEAS CUSTOMERS: Please allow 22p per book.

Whilst every effort is made to keep prices low it is sometimes necessary to increase cover prices at short notice. Angus & Robertson (UK) reserve the right to show new retail prices on covers which may differ from those previously advertised in the text or elsewhere.